GAME CHANGER SPORTS JOURNAL

First edition 2025

ABOUT ME

Name

Age

Height

Sport

Favourite Sportsperson

Inspired By

If Found, Please Contact

CONTENTS

WHY KEEP A SPORTS JOURNAL?

Welcome to this awesome journey of Game Changing growth and success.

We understand the challenges young athletes face as you strive to get better and we're here to help you. **Keeping a journal helps you understand yourself, set exciting goals and navigate the ups and downs of your sports journey**, making you more confident and in control of your progress. It can also give you the edge on being more **resilient**, **focused** and **ready to conquer any challenges** that come your way.

The Game Changer Sports Journal is the perfect place for you to do all of this. You'll discover how to **set effective goals**, **journal your matches or competitions** and **record what you did in training**. Our Game Changer Guidance will not only help you harness the power of your emotions, it will advise you on other aspects of your sport, like looking after yourself and building good relationships with the people around you.

Think of us as your sporting support team. We're here because we believe in your potential as a young athlete and a future 'Game Changer'. As you fill out your journal page by page, you can look back on it with pride and see just how much you've grown and accomplished.

"You can become whatever you want to become, no matter what your background is"

Siya Kolisi

Sport:
Rugby Union

Team/Country:
South Africa Rugby Team

Honours:
2 x World Cup Winner

HOW TO USE YOUR GAME CHANGER SPORTS JOURNAL

Before you get started, let's take a quick look at how the **Game Changer Sports Journal** works...

SET GOALS

Think about what you want to achieve out of your sport and write it down.

KEEP A TRAINING JOURNAL

Track your progress by keeping notes on what you do in training.

KEEP A MATCH/COMPETITION JOURNAL

Before and after each match/competition, write your goals, feelings, what happened and all the best bits!

EMOTIONS

Explore these pages to help deal with how you feel, especially if your emotions are getting in the way of you doing your best.

PERSONAL WELL-BEING

Here you will find techniques to help manage your emotions and feel more ready to perform well.

PHYSICAL WELL-BEING

Discover more resources to help you level-up your sporting journey, from eating well to getting enough rest.

SHOUT-OUTS

When people inspire you, write it down here.

We will show you how to do all of the above with Game Changing examples and explanations to put you on the right track.

“I have short goals - to get better every day, to help my teammates every day - but **my only ultimate goal is to win an NBA championship**. It’s all that matters. I dream about it. I dream about it all the time, how it would look, how it would feel. It would be so amazing”

LeBron James

Sport:	Team/Country:	Honours:
Basketball	**LA Lakers, Team USA**	**4 x NBA Championship Winner**

GOALS

WHY SET GOALS?

It's time for you to set some sporting goals and record them in this section. What skills do you want to improve? What aspects of your performance do you wish to work on? What results are you aiming for? How can you contribute to your team's success?

Setting goals will help you:

STAY FOCUSSED

STAY MOTIVATED

TRACK YOUR PROGRESS

TAKE CONTROL

Setting goals can **enhance your skills** and help you stay on the right track to achieve what you want. You can come back to your goals and change them when you want to make them easier or more challenging. It's also fine not to achieve a goal or decide that one wasn't for you. **Aiming for something and working towards it is a positive move towards being a Game Changer.**

GOAL SETTING TIPS

Before you start setting goals, check out our **G-A-M-E Changer Guidance**. It's your go-to for awesome goal setting:

G

Goals Get Specific

Instead of saying, "I want to be the best player on my team" try, "I want to be the top scorer by the end of the season". Being specific is giving your goal more detail.

A

Achievable Adventures

Aim for challenging but achievable goals in order to improve without getting discouraged. In any case, the result does not matter, it's starting the journey that counts.

M

Mix Short & Long Term

Set goals that will take a short time to complete AND set goals that take longer to accomplish, too. A mix of both keeps you motivated and helps you progress. Under 6 months is a short-term goal; anything more is a long-term goal.

E

Evaluate and Evolve

Keep coming back to look at your goals to help you stay on track. Make notes on any updates you have, and remember that it's OK to make changes to the goals as you go or even decide that a goal is not for you.

Ideas

You can set goals for anything related to your performance or results, whether it's improving your skills, physical fitness or even winning a championship. Now it's your turn.... to help you, look at the examples, then brainstorm your ideas before you complete the goal pages.

GOAL IDEAS

Your goals can be **ANYTHING** you want them to be.
Here are some ideas:

GAME TIME

WINNING THE LEAGUE

DEFENCE

FITNESS

MEDALS

CHAMPION

STRENGTH

BREAKING RECORDS

TOP SCORER

SCHOLARSHIP

SPEED

AWARDS

FIRST TEAM

MY GOAL IDEAS

Before you write out your actual goals on the goal-setting pages, **brainstorm a few goal ideas** and write them here...

Which ones stand out to you? Now you have a few ideas, you are all set to write them down with more detail on your My Goals pages...

"You have to be prepared for a failure to get better"

Lewis Hamilton

Sport:
F1 Racing Driver

Team/Country:
Great Britain

Honours:
7 x F1 World Drivers' Champion

MY GOALS

These next pages are for you to set some sporting goals. Use one page per goal. You can have as many goals as you like. Remember to make your goal specific by adding as much detail as possible.

Date:

Short-term goal ☐ **Long-term goal** ☐

My goal is:

Date:

Short-term goal ☐ Long-term goal ☐

My goal is:

Date:

Short-term goal ☐ **Long-term goal** ☐

My goal is:

Date:

Short-term goal ☐ **Long-term goal** ☐

My goal is:

Date:

Short-term goal ☐ Long-term goal ☐

My goal is:

Date:

Short-term goal ☐ Long-term goal ☐

My goal is:

Date:

Short-term goal ☐ Long-term goal ☐

My goal is:

Date:

Short-term goal ☐ **Long-term goal** ☐

My goal is:

Date:

Short-term goal ☐ **Long-term goal** ☐

My goal is:

"Good teams become great ones when the members trust each other enough to surrender the Me for the We."

Phil Jackson

Sport:
Basketball

Team/Country:
Coach of Chicago Bulls 1989-98

Honours:
11 X NBA Champion

MY TEAM

TEAM PAGE

When everyone works towards a common goal, incredible things can happen. This page is your space to note down those who share the journey with you.

Team name:

Teammates and training buddies:

1.
2.
3.
4.
5.
6.
7.
8.
9.
10.
11.
12.
13.
14.
15.
16.

CREATING POSITIVE VIBES WITH YOUR TEAM

Your teammates and training buddies share each training session with you, making it important to develop positive relationships with them. When Game Changers unite, their combined power can send out shockwaves! These top 10 tips will help strengthen your bonds and unleash the full potential of your squad:

1

Trust

Be reliable, dependable and accountable for your actions. Trust your teammates to do their best, and they will trust you in return.

2

Positive vibes

Create positive vibes within the team. Support and encourage each other, celebrate successes and offer help to teammates who may be struggling.

3

Be a good teammate

Show kindness by supporting your teammates. Encourage and cheer each other on during practices and games/competitions.

4

Communicate

Listen attentively, share your thoughts and communicate clearly. Be open to feedback, and express yourself respectfully.

5

Be a good sport

Show sportsmanship by winning or losing gracefully and treating opponents with respect. Celebrate achievements together, and learn from setbacks as a team.

6

Work together

Collaborate in training sessions by practicing drills and strategies together. Offer support and constructive feedback to help each other improve.

7

Respect

Communicate openly and show respect to your teammates. Make sure it stays a safe and supportive space where everyone feels heard and valued.

8

Teamwork makes the dream work

Understand your role within the team and work together towards common goals. Trust your teammates and rely on each other's strengths.

9

Spend time together

Organise team activities or social events to bond and get to know each other better. Building relationships outside of your sport strengthens teamwork when you come together to perform.

10

Have fun

Remember that sport is not just about winning; it's about the joy of playing and growing together as a team. Cherish the moments, have fun and create lasting memories.

"Practice creates confidence.
Confidence empowers you"

Simone Biles

Sport:
Artistic Gymnastics

Team/Country:
Team USA

Honours:
**6 x All-round World Champion,
2 x All-round Olympic Champion**

TRAINING JOURNAL

STRIVE
SUCCEED
TARGET
REFLECT
ADVANCE

WHY KEEP A TRAINING JOURNAL?

GAME CHANGER GUIDANCE

Keeping training notes can help you become a better athlete in several ways. Look to the S.T.A.R.S Game Changer Guidance to show you why:

S

Strive
Track your progress to strive for improvement.

T

Target
Staying accountable and always targeting your goals will keep you motivated.

A

Advance
Identify areas for improvement to advance your skills as an athlete.

R

Reflect
Express yourself in your training log and reflect on your journey. You can vent and let off steam if you need to!

S

Succeed
Achieve success through this simple process. Look back on your notes and see how far you have come.

HOW TO COMPLETE THE TRAINING JOURNAL

You can use one page per training session. On this page, you will be asked the same questions each time. Firstly, you will put the date, then answer the following questions:

What Did You Do in Training?

Write down the exercises or activities you did during training, and keep a record of what you learnt.

How Did it Go?

Describe how your training session went - was it good, okay or challenging?

How Did You Feel?

Write how you felt during training—happy, tired or excited. Use this space to put down your thoughts or vent if you need to.

Any Thoughts or Aims for the Next Training?

Write down any ideas or areas you'd like to focus on in your next training session. This will give you something to work towards.

By doing the above, you can keep track of your progress, understand your feelings during training and plan for improvement in the future. If your feelings or emotions are holding you back or getting in the way of your training sessions, check out the "What If" section after the Journal pages for some advice.

What did you do in training? **Date:** April 23

Today, I worked on my footwork, coordination and stamina to step up my game.

How did it go?

It was solid. I could feel myself getting smoother with my moves and more in control.

How did you feel?

I felt pretty focused and determined. It's cool to see myself improving and knowing I'm putting in the work.

Any thoughts or aims for the next training?

I wanna keep pushing myself with speed and agility drills next time. Plus, I'm thinking about trying some mental prep stuff from my journal to better prepare for competitions.

"I don't want to be better than you or her or him - I want to be better than I am right now"

Kerri Walsh Jennings

Sport:
Beach Volleyball

Team/Country:
USA

Honours:
3 x Olympic Champion,
3 x World Champion

MY TRAINING JOURNAL

TRAINING JOURNAL

Date:

What did you do in training?

How did it go?

How did you feel?

Any thoughts or aims for the next training?

TRAINING JOURNAL

Date:

What did you do in training?

How did it go?

How did you feel?

Any thoughts or aims for the next training?

TRAINING JOURNAL

Date:

What did you do in training?

How did it go?

How did you feel?

Any thoughts or aims for the next training?

TRAINING JOURNAL

Date:

What did you do in training?

How did it go?

How did you feel?

Any thoughts or aims for the next training?

TRAINING JOURNAL

Date:

What did you do in training?

How did it go?

How did you feel?

Any thoughts or aims for the next training?

TRAINING JOURNAL

Date:

What did you do in training?

How did it go?

How did you feel?

Any thoughts or aims for the next training?

TRAINING JOURNAL

Date:

What did you do in training?

How did it go?

How did you feel?

Any thoughts or aims for the next training?

TRAINING JOURNAL

Date:

What did you do in training?

How did it go?

How did you feel?

Any thoughts or aims for the next training?

TRAINING JOURNAL

Date:

What did you do in training?

How did it go?

How did you feel?

Any thoughts or aims for the next training?

TRAINING JOURNAL

Date:

What did you do in training?

How did it go?

How did you feel?

Any thoughts or aims for the next training?

TRAINING JOURNAL

Date:

What did you do in training?

How did it go?

How did you feel?

Any thoughts or aims for the next training?

TRAINING JOURNAL

Date:

What did you do in training?

How did it go?

How did you feel?

Any thoughts or aims for the next training?

TRAINING JOURNAL

Date:

What did you do in training?

How did it go?

How did you feel?

Any thoughts or aims for the next training?

TRAINING JOURNAL

Date:

What did you do in training?

How did it go?

How did you feel?

Any thoughts or aims for the next training?

TRAINING JOURNAL

Date:

What did you do in training?

How did it go?

How did you feel?

Any thoughts or aims for the next training?

TRAINING JOURNAL

Date:

What did you do in training?

How did it go?

How did you feel?

Any thoughts or aims for the next training?

TRAINING JOURNAL

Date:

What did you do in training?

How did it go?

How did you feel?

Any thoughts or aims for the next training?

TRAINING JOURNAL

Date:

What did you do in training?

How did it go?

How did you feel?

Any thoughts or aims for the next training?

TRAINING JOURNAL

Date:

What did you do in training?

How did it go?

How did you feel?

Any thoughts or aims for the next training?

TRAINING JOURNAL

Date:

What did you do in training?

How did it go?

How did you feel?

Any thoughts or aims for the next training?

TRAINING JOURNAL

Date:

What did you do in training?

How did it go?

How did you feel?

Any thoughts or aims for the next training?

TRAINING JOURNAL

Date:

What did you do in training?

How did it go?

How did you feel?

Any thoughts or aims for the next training?

TRAINING JOURNAL

Date:

What did you do in training?

How did it go?

How did you feel?

Any thoughts or aims for the next training?

TRAINING JOURNAL

Date:

What did you do in training?

How did it go?

How did you feel?

Any thoughts or aims for the next training?

TRAINING JOURNAL

Date:

What did you do in training?

How did it go?

How did you feel?

Any thoughts or aims for the next training?

"It wasn't easy at all, so it just showed us that every team is going to bring it and don't doubt any team. Every game we play, the next game is the biggest game"

Ilona Maher

Sport:
Rugby

Team/Country:
USA

Honours:
Olympic Bronze Medalist

TRAINING JOURNAL

Date:

What did you do in training?

How did it go?

How did you feel?

Any thoughts or aims for the next training?

TRAINING JOURNAL

Date:

What did you do in training?

How did it go?

How did you feel?

Any thoughts or aims for the next training?

TRAINING JOURNAL

Date:

What did you do in training?

How did it go?

How did you feel?

Any thoughts or aims for the next training?

TRAINING JOURNAL

Date:

What did you do in training?

How did it go?

How did you feel?

Any thoughts or aims for the next training?

TRAINING JOURNAL

Date:

What did you do in training?

How did it go?

How did you feel?

Any thoughts or aims for the next training?

TRAINING JOURNAL

Date:

What did you do in training?

How did it go?

How did you feel?

Any thoughts or aims for the next training?

TRAINING JOURNAL

Date:

What did you do in training?

How did it go?

How did you feel?

Any thoughts or aims for the next training?

TRAINING JOURNAL

Date:

What did you do in training?

How did it go?

How did you feel?

Any thoughts or aims for the next training?

TRAINING JOURNAL

Date:

What did you do in training?

How did it go?

How did you feel?

Any thoughts or aims for the next training?

TRAINING JOURNAL

Date:

What did you do in training?

How did it go?

How did you feel?

Any thoughts or aims for the next training?

TRAINING JOURNAL

Date:

What did you do in training?

How did it go?

How did you feel?

Any thoughts or aims for the next training?

TRAINING JOURNAL

Date:

What did you do in training?

How did it go?

How did you feel?

Any thoughts or aims for the next training?

TRAINING JOURNAL

Date:

What did you do in training?

How did it go?

How did you feel?

Any thoughts or aims for the next training?

TRAINING JOURNAL

Date:

What did you do in training?

How did it go?

How did you feel?

Any thoughts or aims for the next training?

TRAINING JOURNAL

Date:

What did you do in training?

How did it go?

How did you feel?

Any thoughts or aims for the next training?

TRAINING JOURNAL

Date:

What did you do in training?

How did it go?

How did you feel?

Any thoughts or aims for the next training?

TRAINING JOURNAL

Date:

What did you do in training?

How did it go?

How did you feel?

Any thoughts or aims for the next training?

TRAINING JOURNAL

Date:

What did you do in training?

How did it go?

How did you feel?

Any thoughts or aims for the next training?

TRAINING JOURNAL

Date:

What did you do in training?

How did it go?

How did you feel?

Any thoughts or aims for the next training?

TRAINING JOURNAL

Date:

What did you do in training?

How did it go?

How did you feel?

Any thoughts or aims for the next training?

TRAINING JOURNAL

Date:

What did you do in training?

How did it go?

How did you feel?

Any thoughts or aims for the next training?

TRAINING JOURNAL

Date:

What did you do in training?

How did it go?

How did you feel?

Any thoughts or aims for the next training?

TRAINING JOURNAL

Date:

What did you do in training?

How did it go?

How did you feel?

Any thoughts or aims for the next training?

TRAINING JOURNAL

Date:

What did you do in training?

How did it go?

How did you feel?

Any thoughts or aims for the next training?

TRAINING JOURNAL

Date:

What did you do in training?

How did it go?

How did you feel?

Any thoughts or aims for the next training?

"Every experience, good or bad, you have to learn from"

Patrick Mahomes

Sport:
American Football

Team/Country:
Kansas City Chiefs

Honours:
3 x NFL Super Bowl Champion

MATCH/ COMPETITION JOURNAL

WHY KEEP A PRE/POST MATCH JOURNAL?

GUIDANCE GAME CHANGER

Dive into Journaling and discover the hidden power of putting pen to paper, unlocking a world where your thoughts and aspirations come to life. Here is the J.O.T.S Game Changer Guidance to show you why journaling is going to change your game for the better...

J

Jot it down
Jot down your thoughts before and after games/ competitions to help you focus.

O

Objectives on paper
Writing match and competition goals down makes them powerful reminders that help to keep you motivated and focused.

T

Turbocharge confidence
Boost your confidence by noting down your positive thoughts and outcomes.

S

Share and reflect
Express yourself and share your feelings in your journal. Reflecting on these pages will help you improve and learn about yourself.

We want you to celebrate your achievements and use your pre and post-match journal to learn and grow.

HOW TO COMPLETE THE PRE-MATCH PAGE

Each time you have a game/competition complete the pre-match page. You can do this a few weeks, a few days or a few hours before the game/competition. The earlier you complete it though, the more time you will have to work on goals for that specific match/competition. **You will need to write down:**

Date, time, venue, etc.

Write down the important details of the match/competition like the date, time and venue. This helps you mentally prepare for the upcoming event.

Your opponent

Take notes on your opponent. Think about their playing style, strengths, and weaknesses. If it's a team, think about how they work together and if there's a standout player. Use insights from previous meetings with them or ask your coach.

Match/competition goals

Set clear goals for the match/competition. What do you want to achieve for yourself or the team? These goals will give you a sense of purpose and focus. Here are a few ideas of some goals:

- Score at least one goal during the match (individual goal)
- Help a teammate to score (team goal)
- Prevent the opponent from scoring (defensive goal)
- Try a new move that I practised in training (skills goal)
- Beat a personal record (desired outcome)

Emotions

Rate your emotions about the upcoming event. Colour-in the circles to show how strong your feelings are—whether it's excitement, nervousness, or confidence. This helps you understand and manage your emotional state during the match or competition. The emotions will be explained next and there is help dealing with those in the Help & Advice section.

Date: April 24 **Time:** 14:00 **Place:** Paxton Gym

Opponent: Springtown Lasers

My goals for this match/competition are:

Score at least 10 points.

Play a big part in the team defence

Be more vocal and communicate effectively with my teammates.

Stay focused, trust my training, and have fun

How I feel before this match/competition:

Confident	●	●	●	●	●	●	●	●	●	○
Excited	●	●	●	●	●	●	○	○	○	○
Nervous	●	●	●	●	●	●	●	●	○	○
Motivated	●	●	●	●	●	●	●	●	●	●

Calm (YES) / NO

YOUR PRE-MATCH EMOTIONS

You are going to be rating your feelings before a match/competition but what do those feelings look like? Here is a quick guide:

CONFIDENCE

You are ready and positive about your skills and sure that you can do well. Your heart is steady and your thoughts are focused.

EXCITEMENT

You are looking forward to participating and eager for action. You might feel a rush of energy and can't wait to start.

NERVOUS

You are a bit worried or are stressing about what is ahead. You might have butterflies in your stomach or feel a little tense.

MOTIVATION

You are eager to do well, try your best and work hard to succeed. You might have a burst of energy and determination.

CALM

You are feeling peaceful, relaxed, clear and composed. Your breathing is steady and your body feels at ease.

What if some of these feelings are overwhelming or getting in the way of your performance? We are here for you! Read on...

If you're gearing up for a big match/competition, it's perfectly normal for your emotions to go up and down. After all, having a mix of feelings is just a natural part of competing in sports.

Whether you prefer handling these emotions yourself or by chatting with those around you, it's entirely up to you. However, if you find that your emotions are affecting your performance in a negative way or how you want to perform, don't worry, our Game Changer Guidance is here to give you ways to navigate the range of emotions you might have.

Following your match/competition journal pages, you'll find the "What if..." section which is a resource you can turn to at ANY TIME for help. This section is designed to help you unravel all those feelings to get the most out of your performance in upcoming matches/competitions. Here's what's covered....

What if I am lacking in confidence? Turn to page 149

What if I'm not that into it? Turn to page 150

What if I'm not feeling any emotion? Turn to page 151

What if I am feeling worried or nervous? Turn to page 153

This targeted advice aims to empower you, ensuring you stay on track to make the most of your big moment.

HOW TO COMPLETE THE POST-MATCH PAGE

Complete your post-match/competition page after EVERY performance. It can help you understand how you did, feel good about what went well and get ready for the next time. Here is what you need to write down:

Result

Write down what happened in the match—whether you won, lost, or if it was a draw. You can look back at this to remember the experience.

How did you feel about the match/competition?

Write down how you felt emotionally after the performance....happy, sad, excited, or any other emotion.

Did you achieve your goals?

Check if you did the things you planned to do in the pre-match/competition page and write how you got on here. It's okay not to achieve everything. What is important is that there was something to aim for.

Good things about the match/competition

Note anything positive or good that happened during the match/competition. Recognising the good stuff (however big or small) helps you learn and improve.

Would you change anything?

Think about what you might want to do differently next time, What will you work on before the next match/competition? Write down the areas you want to get better so you can keep improving and reaching your goals.

Result/score:

We totally nailed it 65-52 !!

How do you feel about the match/competition?

I'm buzzing! It was intense, but pulling off the win feels unreal.

Did you achieve your match/competition goals?

Absolutely! I hit my target of 12 points, hustled for 3 steals, and communicated well with everyone.

What were the good things about the match/competition?

Our teamwork was fire! Everyone had each other's backs, and we ran our plays like in training. Offense was smooth, and we hustled hard on D.

Would you change anything?

Definitely gotta tighten up our shooting. We missed a few easy shots that could've got us a better lead.

What do you plan to work on before your next match/competition?

Gonna practice my shooting. Also, gonna do better on my defence and be more agressive. Can't let up for a second in the next game!

YOU'RE ALL SET!

Now you have set your goals and you know what to do, it's time to start your match/competition journaling! Don't forget after the journal section you will find the Help & Advice part that will help you with emotions, self-care and physical well being like eating healthily and dealing with injuries.

"Champions keep playing until they get it right"

Billie Jean King

Sport: **Tennis**

Team/Country: **USA**

Honours: **12 x Grand Slam Singles Titles**

MY MATCH/ COMPETITION JOURNAL

PRE-MATCH JOURNAL

Date:	Time:	Place:

Opponent:

My goals for this match/competition are:

How I feel before this match/competition:

Confident	○	○	○	○	○	○	○	○	○	○
Excited	○	○	○	○	○	○	○	○	○	○
Nervous	○	○	○	○	○	○	○	○	○	○
Motivated	○	○	○	○	○	○	○	○	○	○
Calm	**YES / NO**									

POST-MATCH JOURNAL

Result/score:

How do you feel about the match/competition?

Did you achieve your match/competition goals?

What were the good things about the match/competition?

Would you change anything?

What do you plan to work on before your next match/ competition?

PRE-MATCH JOURNAL

Date:

Time: Place:

Opponent:

My goals for this match/competition are:

How I feel before this match/competition:

Confident	○	○	○	○	○	○	○	○	○	○
Excited	○	○	○	○	○	○	○	○	○	○
Nervous	○	○	○	○	○	○	○	○	○	○
Motivated	○	○	○	○	○	○	○	○	○	○

Calm YES / NO

POST-MATCH JOURNAL

Result/score:

How do you feel about the match/competition?

Did you achieve your match/competition goals?

What were the good things about the match/competition?

Would you change anything?

What do you plan to work on before your next match/ competition?

PRE-MATCH JOURNAL

Date:	Time:	Place:

Opponent:

My goals for this match/competition are:

How I feel before this match/competition:

Confident	◯	◯	◯	◯	◯	◯	◯	◯	◯	◯
Excited	◯	◯	◯	◯	◯	◯	◯	◯	◯	◯
Nervous	◯	◯	◯	◯	◯	◯	◯	◯	◯	◯
Motivated	◯	◯	◯	◯	◯	◯	◯	◯	◯	◯

Calm **YES / NO**

POST-MATCH JOURNAL

Result/score:

How do you feel about the match/competition?

Did you achieve your match/competition goals?

What were the good things about the match/competition?

Would you change anything?

What do you plan to work on before your next match/competition?

PRE-MATCH JOURNAL

Date:

Time: Place:

Opponent:

My goals for this match/competition are:

How I feel before this match/competition:

Confident	○	○	○	○	○	○	○	○	○	○
Excited	○	○	○	○	○	○	○	○	○	○
Nervous	○	○	○	○	○	○	○	○	○	○
Motivated	○	○	○	○	○	○	○	○	○	○

Calm YES / NO

POST-MATCH JOURNAL

Result/score:

How do you feel about the match/competition?

Did you achieve your match/competition goals?

What were the good things about the match/competition?

Would you change anything?

What do you plan to work on before your next match/ competition?

PRE-MATCH JOURNAL

Date:

Time: **Place:**

Opponent:

My goals for this match/competition are:

How I feel before this match/competition:

Confident	○	○	○	○	○	○	○	○	○	○
Excited	○	○	○	○	○	○	○	○	○	○
Nervous	○	○	○	○	○	○	○	○	○	○
Motivated	○	○	○	○	○	○	○	○	○	○

Calm **YES / NO**

POST-MATCH JOURNAL

Result/score:

How do you feel about the match/competition?

Did you achieve your match/competition goals?

What were the good things about the match/competition?

Would you change anything?

What do you plan to work on before your next match/competition?

PRE-MATCH JOURNAL

Date:	Time:	Place:

Opponent:

My goals for this match/competition are:

How I feel before this match/competition:

Confident	○	○	○	○	○	○	○	○	○	○
Excited	○	○	○	○	○	○	○	○	○	○
Nervous	○	○	○	○	○	○	○	○	○	○
Motivated	○	○	○	○	○	○	○	○	○	○

Calm **YES / NO**

POST-MATCH JOURNAL

Result/score:

How do you feel about the match/competition?

Did you achieve your match/competition goals?

What were the good things about the match/competition?

Would you change anything?

What do you plan to work on before your next match/competition?

PRE-MATCH JOURNAL

Date:

Time: **Place:**

Opponent:

My goals for this match/competition are:

How I feel before this match/competition:

Confident ○ ○ ○ ○ ○ ○ ○ ○ ○ ○

Excited ○ ○ ○ ○ ○ ○ ○ ○ ○ ○

Nervous ○ ○ ○ ○ ○ ○ ○ ○ ○ ○

Motivated ○ ○ ○ ○ ○ ○ ○ ○ ○ ○

Calm **YES / NO**

POST-MATCH JOURNAL

Result/score:

How do you feel about the match/competition?

Did you achieve your match/competition goals?

What were the good things about the match/competition?

Would you change anything?

What do you plan to work on before your next match/ competition?

PRE-MATCH JOURNAL

Date:

Time: **Place:**

Opponent:

My goals for this match/competition are:

How I feel before this match/competition:

Confident	○	○	○	○	○	○	○	○	○	○
Excited	○	○	○	○	○	○	○	○	○	○
Nervous	○	○	○	○	○	○	○	○	○	○
Motivated	○	○	○	○	○	○	○	○	○	○

Calm **YES / NO**

POST-MATCH JOURNAL

Result/score:

How do you feel about the match/competition?

Did you achieve your match/competition goals?

What were the good things about the match/competition?

Would you change anything?

What do you plan to work on before your next match/ competition?

PRE-MATCH JOURNAL

Date:

Time: **Place:**

Opponent:

My goals for this match/competition are:

How I feel before this match/competition:

Confident ○ ○ ○ ○ ○ ○ ○ ○ ○ ○

Excited ○ ○ ○ ○ ○ ○ ○ ○ ○ ○

Nervous ○ ○ ○ ○ ○ ○ ○ ○ ○ ○

Motivated ○ ○ ○ ○ ○ ○ ○ ○ ○ ○

Calm **YES / NO**

POST-MATCH JOURNAL

Result/score:

How do you feel about the match/competition?

Did you achieve your match/competition goals?

What were the good things about the match/competition?

Would you change anything?

What do you plan to work on before your next match/ competition?

PRE-MATCH JOURNAL

Date:

Time: Place:

Opponent:

My goals for this match/competition are:

How I feel before this match/competition:

Confident	○	○	○	○	○	○	○	○	○	○
Excited	○	○	○	○	○	○	○	○	○	○
Nervous	○	○	○	○	○	○	○	○	○	○
Motivated	○	○	○	○	○	○	○	○	○	○

Calm YES / NO

POST-MATCH JOURNAL

Result/score:

How do you feel about the match/competition?

Did you achieve your match/competition goals?

What were the good things about the match/competition?

Would you change anything?

What do you plan to work on before your next match/ competition?

PRE-MATCH JOURNAL

Date:

Time: **Place:**

Opponent:

My goals for this match/competition are:

How I feel before this match/competition:

Confident	○	○	○	○	○	○	○	○	○	○
Excited	○	○	○	○	○	○	○	○	○	○
Nervous	○	○	○	○	○	○	○	○	○	○
Motivated	○	○	○	○	○	○	○	○	○	○

Calm **YES / NO**

POST-MATCH JOURNAL

Result/score:

How do you feel about the match/competition?

Did you achieve your match/competition goals?

What were the good things about the match/competition?

Would you change anything?

What do you plan to work on before your next match/competition?

PRE-MATCH JOURNAL

Date:

Time: **Place:**

Opponent:

My goals for this match/competition are:

How I feel before this match/competition:

Confident	○	○	○	○	○	○	○	○	○	○
Excited	○	○	○	○	○	○	○	○	○	○
Nervous	○	○	○	○	○	○	○	○	○	○
Motivated	○	○	○	○	○	○	○	○	○	○

Calm **YES / NO**

POST-MATCH JOURNAL

Result/score:

How do you feel about the match/competition?

Did you achieve your match/competition goals?

What were the good things about the match/competition?

Would you change anything?

What do you plan to work on before your next match/competition?

PRE-MATCH JOURNAL

Date:

Time: **Place:**

Opponent:

My goals for this match/competition are:

How I feel before this match/competition:

Confident	○	○	○	○	○	○	○	○	○	○
Excited	○	○	○	○	○	○	○	○	○	○
Nervous	○	○	○	○	○	○	○	○	○	○
Motivated	○	○	○	○	○	○	○	○	○	○

Calm **YES / NO**

POST-MATCH JOURNAL

Result/score:

How do you feel about the match/competition?

Did you achieve your match/competition goals?

What were the good things about the match/competition?

Would you change anything?

What do you plan to work on before your next match/competition?

PRE-MATCH JOURNAL

Date:

Time: Place:

Opponent:

My goals for this match/competition are:

How I feel before this match/competition:

Confident	○	○	○	○	○	○	○	○	○	○
Excited	○	○	○	○	○	○	○	○	○	○
Nervous	○	○	○	○	○	○	○	○	○	○
Motivated	○	○	○	○	○	○	○	○	○	○

Calm YES / NO

POST-MATCH JOURNAL

Result/score:

How do you feel about the match/competition?

Did you achieve your match/competition goals?

What were the good things about the match/competition?

Would you change anything?

What do you plan to work on before your next match/competition?

PRE-MATCH JOURNAL

Date:

Time: **Place:**

Opponent:

My goals for this match/competition are:

How I feel before this match/competition:

Confident ○ ○ ○ ○ ○ ○ ○ ○ ○ ○

Excited ○ ○ ○ ○ ○ ○ ○ ○ ○ ○

Nervous ○ ○ ○ ○ ○ ○ ○ ○ ○ ○

Motivated ○ ○ ○ ○ ○ ○ ○ ○ ○ ○

Calm **YES / NO**

POST-MATCH JOURNAL

Result/score:

How do you feel about the match/competition?

Did you achieve your match/competition goals?

What were the good things about the match/competition?

Would you change anything?

What do you plan to work on before your next match/competition?

PRE-MATCH JOURNAL

Date:

Time: **Place:**

Opponent:

My goals for this match/competition are:

How I feel before this match/competition:

Confident ○ ○ ○ ○ ○ ○ ○ ○ ○ ○

Excited ○ ○ ○ ○ ○ ○ ○ ○ ○ ○

Nervous ○ ○ ○ ○ ○ ○ ○ ○ ○ ○

Motivated ○ ○ ○ ○ ○ ○ ○ ○ ○ ○

Calm YES / NO

POST-MATCH JOURNAL

Result/score:

How do you feel about the match/competition?

Did you achieve your match/competition goals?

What were the good things about the match/competition?

Would you change anything?

What do you plan to work on before your next match/ competition?

PRE-MATCH JOURNAL

Date:

Time: **Place:**

Opponent:

My goals for this match/competition are:

How I feel before this match/competition:

Confident	◯	◯	◯	◯	◯	◯	◯	◯	◯	◯
Excited	◯	◯	◯	◯	◯	◯	◯	◯	◯	◯
Nervous	◯	◯	◯	◯	◯	◯	◯	◯	◯	◯
Motivated	◯	◯	◯	◯	◯	◯	◯	◯	◯	◯

Calm **YES / NO**

POST-MATCH JOURNAL

Result/score:

How do you feel about the match/competition?

Did you achieve your match/competition goals?

What were the good things about the match/competition?

Would you change anything?

What do you plan to work on before your next match/ competition?

PRE-MATCH JOURNAL

Date:

Time: **Place:**

Opponent:

My goals for this match/competition are:

How I feel before this match/competition:

Confident	◯	◯	◯	◯	◯	◯	◯	◯	◯	◯
Excited	◯	◯	◯	◯	◯	◯	◯	◯	◯	◯
Nervous	◯	◯	◯	◯	◯	◯	◯	◯	◯	◯
Motivated	◯	◯	◯	◯	◯	◯	◯	◯	◯	◯

Calm **YES / NO**

POST-MATCH JOURNAL

Result/score:

How do you feel about the match/competition?

Did you achieve your match/competition goals?

What were the good things about the match/competition?

Would you change anything?

What do you plan to work on before your next match/ competition?

PRE-MATCH JOURNAL

Date:

Time: Place:

Opponent:

My goals for this match/competition are:

How I feel before this match/competition:

Confident	○	○	○	○	○	○	○	○	○	○
Excited	○	○	○	○	○	○	○	○	○	○
Nervous	○	○	○	○	○	○	○	○	○	○
Motivated	○	○	○	○	○	○	○	○	○	○

Calm YES / NO

POST-MATCH JOURNAL

Result/score:

How do you feel about the match/competition?

Did you achieve your match/competition goals?

What were the good things about the match/competition?

Would you change anything?

What do you plan to work on before your next match/ competition?

PRE-MATCH JOURNAL

Date:

Time: **Place:**

Opponent:

My goals for this match/competition are:

How I feel before this match/competition:

Confident	○	○	○	○	○	○	○	○	○	○
Excited	○	○	○	○	○	○	○	○	○	○
Nervous	○	○	○	○	○	○	○	○	○	○
Motivated	○	○	○	○	○	○	○	○	○	○

Calm **YES / NO**

POST-MATCH JOURNAL

Result/score:

How do you feel about the match/competition?

Did you achieve your match/competition goals?

What were the good things about the match/competition?

Would you change anything?

What do you plan to work on before your next match/competition?

"The only one that can tell you that you can't win - is you, and you don't have to listen"

Jessica Ennis-Hill

Sport:
Athletics

Team/Country:
Great Britain

Honours:
Olympic Champion, European Champion and 3 x World Champion

HELP + ADVICE

WHAT IF?

What if you aren't feeling ready to perform? Reflect on your pre-match/competition emotions... if you're low on motivation, stressed or lacking confidence, these pages are designed to assist in managing those pre-performance feelings. After reading this advice, you can turn to the Personal Well-Being section to try some techniques that might help. All this advice can also be valuable if you're experiencing emotions before training or practice.

WHAT IF...

I'M LACKING IN CONFIDENCE?

If you've rated your confidence low on your journal page, it's very common, and we all feel this way sometimes. Facing a tough opponent can often lead to this feeling before a match, competition or training. Here are some tips to help boost your self-confidence and get you ready for action:

Positive self-talk
Use positive self-talk* by reminding yourself that you have the skills. Stay positive by using phrases like, "I can do it" or, "I've worked hard". This boosts your self-confidence.

Visualisation
Try visualisation* before the match/competition/training or in the days leading up to it, even just for a few minutes. This is where you imagine yourself successfully making great plays to help your team or using the best techniques you learnt in training.

Believe in yourself
Think about everything you've learnt and practiced up until now. You've put in the effort, and your skills are solid – trust in your training, and believe in yourself.

Deep breathing
To stay calm under this pressure, use deep breathing* and progressive muscle relaxation* techniques.

Trial and error
You might not need to spend a lot of time on each of these techniques, and maybe you prefer one over another. Go with what you feel works for you and gives you the best result.

*look up how to do this in the 'personal well-being' section

WHAT IF...

I'M NOT INTO IT?

If your motivation or excitement levels are running low as you approach your next game or competition and the thought of your upcoming training session doesn't quite spark your interest, don't worry! To ignite more enthusiasm, here are some helpful tips:

Reasons why
What's taking away your joy? Take a moment to consider what might be influencing your mood. You engage in your sport because you love it and that should always be the main focus. Never forget why you started in the first place.

Talk it out
Talk to your teammates about how you feel and what they expect from the match/competition or training. You could also share your feelings with the people who know you best, like friends or family. Talking it out can make you feel more connected and ready to perform.

Put on some tunes
Before the match/competition or training, play your favourite music*. Find some uplifting tunes that give you energy and get you in the mood.

Get inspired
Follow professional athletes or teams you admire and even check out some footage of them in action. This will help reignite your passion for your next match, competition or training session.

Set goals
Use your journal to set personal goals before you meet your next opponent. Also re-visit your sporting goals to remind yourself what you want to achieve over the next few months/sessions.

What works for you?
Don't forget that figuring out what works best for you can really change how you feel before you train or compete. So, try out different approaches and stay open to what inspires you the most.

*look up how to do this in the 'personal well-being' section

WHAT IF...

I DON'T FEEL ANY EMOTION?

If you don't feel a lot of emotion about your next match/competition or training don't worry. Every sportsperson manages their emotions differently. It's perfectly acceptable to not feel anything or not know how to describe how you feel. Here are some tips to mentally prepare you for when you don't have strong emotions:

Do nothing; enjoy the moment
You might be just fine as you are, which is totally okay. In which case, just enjoy the moment and do your best in the match/competition or training. If all is well, there is no need to read the rest of the advice! However, if you feel a little flat, then read on...

Stay positive
Even without strong emotions, maintaining a positive mindset is like a super power. Remind yourself of past achievements and focus on the opportunities ahead.

Connect with teammates
Seize the chance to connect with your teammates. Share positive vibes, talk about strategies and create a supportive team atmosphere. If someone's feeling really nervous, be the teammate who lifts their spirits and brings out the best in them.

Watch it

Find some clips or videos to watch online of past matches or highlights. Watching great performances and hearing supporters cheering can inspire you and give you the “buzz” to perform at your best!

Dont hold back

Embrace the lack of strong emotions as a chance to play or train with a clear mind, free from unnecessary pressure. Find the method that works for you to prepare before a game, and stick with it. If it's effective, there is no need to change.

WHAT IF...

I'M FEELING WORRIED OR NERVOUS?

If you are worried, stressed or scared about your next match, competition or training session, don't worry. This happens to most athletes at some point. To reduce these feelings before you go, follow these tips:

Choose your path

Feeling nervous or excited before a game is normal because both feelings wake up the nervous system in a similar way. How it affects you depends on how you see it—like choosing between a 'positive' or 'negative' journey. If you're nervous, try focusing on the good things that can happen in the game, competition, or training. Check out the "Stress Less Page" for some helpful tips the moment you feel nervous.

Get creative

Take your mind off the nerves and take a break. If the butterflies are too much, try creative expression* like colouring, doodling or reading.

Open up

Talk to your coach, parents or a trusted teammate if you need some support. You might find a teammate that feels exactly the same as you, and you can help each other.

Focus on the right things

Focus on what you can control, like your own performance and helping your team or club, rather than things you can't control, such as referees, judges, spectators, the venue or the weather.

Find your zen

Try mindfulness exercises, like deep breathing* or meditation*, the morning of or days leading up to the match, competition or training. It relaxes your mind while helping you focus. It might take some getting used to but it could be the perfect exercise for you.

It's not just me

Feeling worried, nervous or scared is part of performing and preparing to meet your opponent. So, always remember that you are not alone!

We are all different

Our feelings can be stronger and last longer than others. We could be feeling stress or nerves or a mix of both of them. It's okay and completely normal, so try some of the above techniques and see which works best for you. Remember, you always have your coach, teammates and friends to support you.

*look up how to do this in the 'personal well-being' section

THE STRESS LESS PAGE

If you are worried, stressed or scared about training, a match or a competition, it's time for ACTION! Remember that on the "What if I'm Worried..." page we talked about how feelings of nervousness and excitement are from the same reaction in your body? We can take some steps to help change the outcome for you. So, if you are feeling nervous right now, quickly focus on the things that CAN go well for you and write them down on the next page. Below, you can see some examples:

I'm stressed/nervous about:

playing badly today

EXAMPLE GAME CHANGER

Three things that could go right are:

1. *I play well today*
2. *I score more than I ever did*
3. *We win!*

I'm stressed/nervous about:

Training in the top group, not knowing anyone, doing it wrong

Three things that could go right are:

1. *I learn from the experience*
2. *I meet someone new*
3. *I might enjoy it*

I’m stressed/nervous about:

Three things that could go right are:

1.

2.

3.

I’m stressed/nervous about:

Three things that could go right are:

1.

2.

3.

I’m stressed/nervous about:

Three things that could go right are:

1.

2.

3.

"Courage doesn't mean you don't get afraid. Courage means you don't let fears stop you"

Bethany Hamilton

Sport:
Surfing

Team/Country:
USA

Honours:
Champion Surfer

HELP + ADVICE

PERSONAL WELL-BEING

Whether it's feeling jittery before a big day, struggling with self-doubt or simply trying to find a sense of calm amidst the chaos of doing your sport, we've got your back. Our tips and strategies are designed to empower you to stay focused, do your best and enjoy what you love.

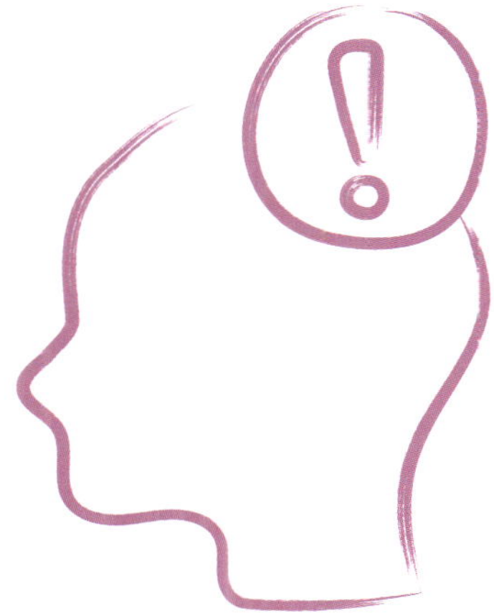

We understand that sporting competitions can stir up various emotions, so our aim is to equip you with the tools to navigate those moments with greater confidence. However you rated your emotions in the pre-match pages, you can find a technique here to help you.

Remember, you're not alone in this. Many other sports people face similar challenges and practice different techniques to overcome them. So let's dive into this section and discover ways to conquer stress, anxiety and nerves like a champion Game Changer.

PROGRESSIVE MUSCLE RELAXATION

What is it?

Progressive muscle relaxation helps you relax by tensing and releasing muscles in different parts of your body. It's a way to reduce stress and give you a sense of calm.

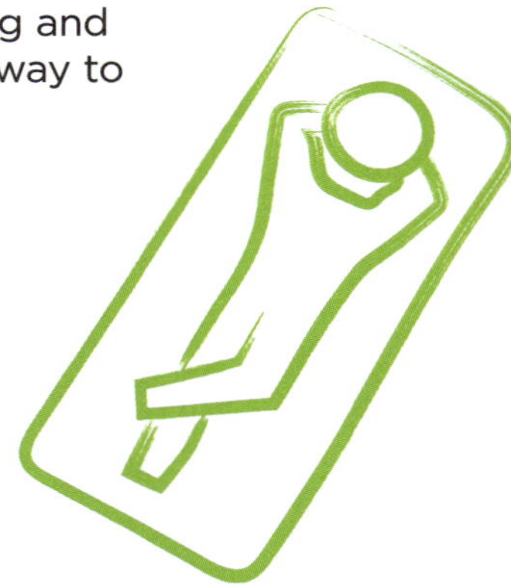

How do I do it?

1 Find a quiet spot and get comfortable.

2 Close your eyes (if you want) and take slow, deep breaths.

3 Start with your feet. Tense them and scrunch up your toes gently for a few seconds, then let them relax. Repeat this a few times.

4 Next, try the same with just your legs. Tense your leg muscles for a few seconds, then let go and feel your legs relax. Repeat this a few times.

5 Next, try your stomach. Tense your stomach muscles for a few seconds, then release them and relax. Repeat this a few times.

6 Now do the same with your arms. Clench your fist and tense your whole arm, then let go and relax. Repeat this a few times.

7 You can even try your face. Scrunch up your face for a moment, then let it relax.

8 Finally, imagine a wave of relaxation flowing from your head to your toes. Take a few more deep breaths and open your eyes when you're ready. Repeat it all again if you want.

MINDFUL MEDITATION

What is it?

Mindful meditation is a special way of focusing your attention and being aware of what's happening right now. It's like training your mind to be really present in the moment. This can be useful before competitive sport because it can help manage emotions, improve concentration, reduce stress and get to know yourself better.

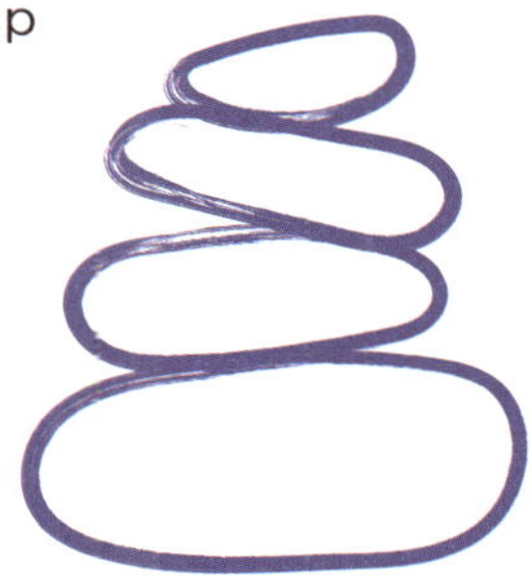

How do I do it?

1. Find a quiet and comfy spot.
2. Get in a comfortable position and close your eyes (if you want).
3. Take slow, deep breaths.
4. While you do this, notice your thoughts like clouds floating by.
5. Focus on your breath going in and out.
6. If your mind wanders it does not matter at all, gently gain focus on your breathing again if you can and continue.
7. You can do this for one/two minutes or more. You might do it for a little longer each time you try as you get more used to it.

Meditation helps you relax, focus and feel calm. It's like giving your mind a break to recharge. Practice it and see how it feels for you.

CREATIVE EXPRESSION

What is it?

Creative expression is a way to relax and have fun before training, a game, or a competition. It means doing activities that let you be creative and express yourself. It's a cool way to calm your mind, take your thoughts off what is ahead, but still be ready to start when the time comes. You will not use too much energy doing any of these activities, so you can save it all for your performance.

How do I do it?

1. **Drawing or Painting**: Use paper and colours to draw or paint whatever you like.

2. **Writing or Journaling**: Use your Game Changer Sports Journal to write down your thoughts about the game, or grab a notebook and try some creative writing.

3. **Music**: Play an instrument or listen to music

4. **Crafts or DIY Projects**: Make something with your hands, like a collage or banner. It can be connected to your sport or totally unrelated.

5. **Mindful Colouring**: Get stuck in to some mandala colouring books to relax and focus your mind.

POSITIVE SELF-TALK

What is it?

Positive self-talk is a way of speaking to yourself in a kind and encouraging way. It involves using positive words and thoughts to boost your confidence, motivate yourself and have more self-belief during the build-up to your game or competition.

How do I do it?

1. **Replace negative thoughts**: When you think something negative, like, *"I can't do it"*, change it to something positive, such as *"I can do it if I try"*.

2. **Encourage yourself**: Use positive words to cheer yourself on, like, *"I am strong and capable"*.

3. **Focus on your strengths**: Think about what you're good at, and remind yourself of past successes. Say things like, *"I am a skilled player"*, or, *"I've worked hard for this"*.

4. **Imagine doing well**: Positive self-talk goes well with visualisation. Check out the visualisation page to see how that can help, too.

Positive self-talk is about changing the way you think and cheering yourself on. It might take some practice to make this change. Give it a try before a game/competition or training session and you should feel the benefits. Keep in mind that you wouldn't criticise a friend or teammate , so avoid doing the same to yourself.

DEEP BREATHING

What is it?

Deep breathing is a simple and powerful way to help calm your body and mind before training, a game, or a competition. It involves taking slow, deep breaths in a controlled and mindful way, helping your body to relax by activating its natural relaxation response. It can calm you down if you are over-excited and reduce feelings of stress and anxiety.

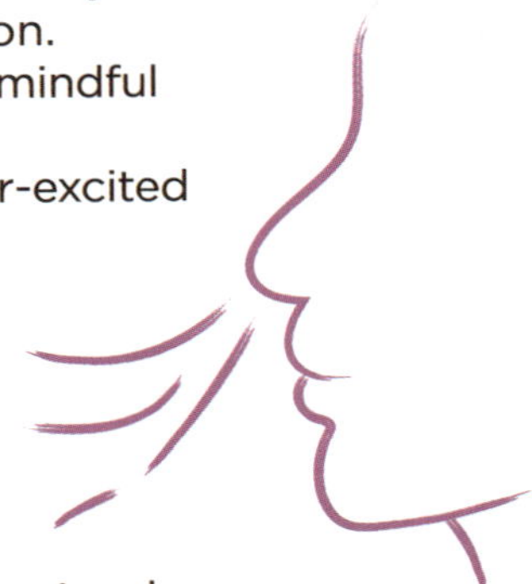

How do I do it?

1. Find a quiet and comfortable spot to sit or stand.

2. Take a slow breath in through your nose, filling your belly with air. Imagine that you are inflating a balloon in your stomach. Feel your stomach inflate.

3. Hold your breath for a moment.

4. Slowly exhale through your mouth, completely letting the air out. Feel your stomach deflate.

5. Repeat this process for as long as you like, taking slow and deep breaths in and out. Notice the air inflate and deflate your stomach each time.

You can do deep breathing whenever you feel the need. It might be the day before or the morning of training, a big match, or a competition. You could even be in the changing room before you step out to play or perform. Deep breathing is simple and easy and can work wonders when you feel nervous or stressed.

VISUALISATION

What is it?

Visualisation is like creating a movie in your mind where you imagine yourself playing or performing successfully. It helps your brain prepare for the competition ahead by creating positive mental images. This can boost your confidence and improve your skills.

How do I do it?

1. Choose your moment. It could be a quiet moment at home, in the changing room before your match/competition or even during your warm-up.

2. Imagine doing your sport in your mind. See yourself out there, either by yourself or with your teammates or opponents.

3. Picture yourself doing all the things you want to do, like making good choices, being successful and performing well.

4. Make the pictures in your mind as clear and detailed as possible.

5. Do this as often as you like for a few minutes or more.

Visualising your goals is also incredibly powerful. These could be goals you set for your next match/competition or the goals that you wrote in the "My Goals" section. Get into your visualisation groove and this can really become your super power.

THE POWER OF MUSIC

How can music help you prepare for sport?

Did you know that music can be your secret weapon to rock your performance and get in the zone? The beats, rhythm and lyrics of your favourite tunes can get you pumped up and ready to conquer. It's like having your personal soundtrack to supercharge your passion! Here are some ways it can help:

CONFIDENCE !!

FOCUS

MOTIVATION

REDUCE STRESS

When is the best time to listen to music?

You can listen to music before stepping out for the warm-up. If you're feeling nervous, try listening to calmer music, as it can help you relax and find your zen. Listening to music in the few days leading up to the game/competition or training can help you stay focused, motivated and mentally prepared.

DONT FORGET!

Music can't replace your physical warm-up routine before you do your sport, so you still need to warm up your body properly. If listening to music before a match/competition or training distracts you or interferes with your focus, it might not be the best strategy for you.

MY GAME CHANGER PLAYLIST

Let's create your ultimate playlist to get in the zone for your best performance. Put your top tune in "now playing".

MY GAME CHANGER PLAYLIST

NOW PLAYING

"Ask not what your teammates can do for you. Ask what you can do for your teammates"

Magic Johnson

Sport:	Team/Country:	Honours:
Basketball	**LA Lakers (1979-91, 1996), Team USA a.k.a. "The Dream Team" (1992)**	**5 x NBA Champion Olympic Champion**

BE A HELPING HAND

Helping out teammates when they are nervous or lacking in confidence is like being a Game Changer superhero. When you support others, it not only makes the team stronger but also boosts your own confidence. It's like passing on positive vibes - when you share, you get back even more. Plus, it's a cool way to show leadership and build a team that's ready for anything. So, lend a hand, be a great teammate and watch how it powers up your own mental game.

OFFER ENCOURAGEMENT

SHARE POSITIVE AFFIRMATIONS

BE A GOOD LISTENER

PRACTICE TOGETHER

CREATE A TEAMMATE RITUAL

CREATE A SUPPORTIVE SPACE

INCLUDE EVERYONE

CELEBRATE SMALL WINS

POSITIVE VIBES WITH MY COACH

Building a good relationship with your coach can be an extra power-up on your sporting journey. Coaches often pour their passion and energy into their team's success, and having a good connection with them can help your personal development and growth in the sport you love. These top 5 tips can help you along the way:

1

RESPECT
Listen in training, follow instructions, and appreciate your coach's efforts.

2

COMMITMENT
Attend training regularly, be on time and give your best effort. This will show your coach how serious you are.

3

COMMUNICATION
If you have something to share, do this respectfully and at an appropriate time.

4

ACCEPTANCE
Embrace constructive criticism as an opportunity to improve.

5

GRATITUDE
Say thank you and appreciate your coach's guidance. A small thank you can go a long way!

WHAT IF I DON'T GET ALONG WITH MY COACH

Sometimes, we might face a challenge with our coach. This could happen because you and your coach have different ideas about how to approach your sport. Differences could possibly be over playing time, game or competition strategies, or styles of performance, but most of the time, these issues are simple to resolve. If you ever find yourself in such a situation, here's a plan to help you tackle it like a Game Changer:

Stay calm
Take a deep breath, and try to stay calm, even if you're upset. Stay cool.

Listen carefully
Pay attention, and try to understand your coach's point of view. Listen well.

Talk to your coach
Find a good time to talk to your coach respectfully. Share how you feel and what you want to resolve.

Find a solution together
Work with your coach to find a way that works for both of you. Think of ideas and be willing to compromise.

Get help if needed
If the situation does not improve, ask a trusted adult, like a parent or guardian, for advice.

Stay focused on your sport
Remember to enjoy the games and competitions, practice hard and be a good team player, even if there are difficulties.

Show respect and be fair
Treat your coach with respect, follow their instructions, and always be a good sport.

TIPS

If you face challenges with your coach, it's a chance to learn and grow. Stay confident, communicate openly and keep your passion alive.

"Worrying gets you nowhere. If you turn up worrying about how you're going to perform, you've already lost. Train hard, turn up, run your best and the rest will take care of itself."

Usain Bolt

Sport:
Athletics

Team/Country:
Jamaica

Honours:
8 x Olympic Gold Medalist, 11 x World Champion, World Record Holder

HELP + ADVICE

PHYSICAL WELL-BEING

INJURIES

When it comes to sporting injuries, even the toughest Game Changers can face challenges. Don't worry, there are some simple strategies to help your body and mind to reignite your game. Check out the advice below to revive your strength and make an epic return after injury.

Stay positive and keep a good attitude. Remember that injuries happen, but you can still come back stronger and better than before.

Talk to your coach, parents or teammates about how you're feeling. They can give you support and encouragement.

Focus on things you can do, like exercises that don't involve the injured area, to maintain your physical fitness and prepare for when you're able to participate again.

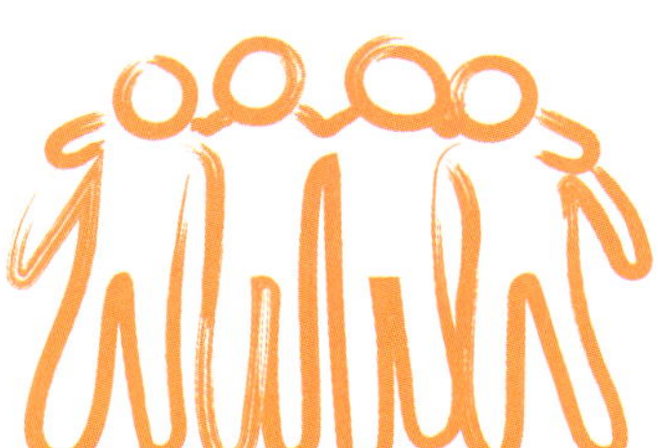

Stay involved with the team, even if you have to take time off from playing. You can still watch training and games/competitions to support your teammates.

WHAT SHOULD YOU DO IF YOU'RE INJURED

Injuries can be tough, but taking care of yourself is really important. Here's what you should do if you get hurt:

Rest Up
Give your body the time it needs to heal. It's okay to take it easy.

Get Expert Help
Talk to a doctor or Physiotherapist to find out how serious the injury is and what you should do.

Follow the Plan
Stick to the recovery plan they give you to get back on track.

Update Your Coach
Let your coach know about your injury and how long you might be out. They'll understand and can help you with your return.

Stay in Touch
Keep going to training and games to support your team and stay connected, even if you can't play.

TIPS

It can be frustrating to have an injury and not be able to do anything for a while. It's completely normal to feel upset, disappointed or left out. Remember, it's important to stay positive, be patient and follow the advice you have been given so you can return to the game fully recovered.

INJURY RECORD

Are you injured? Don't worry! This is your space to write freely about what happened, your recovery plan, vent your feelings or simply doodle while you recover....

HEALTHY EATING

What you eat and drink is super important for how well you feel emotionally and how you perform each time. By eating healthily, you can help your body stay energised and strong whilst keeping your mind focused. Check out these tips to help you eat like a Game Changer and unleash your best performance:

Eat a balanced diet that includes plenty of fruits, vegetables, whole grains, lean proteins, like eggs or white meat, and healthy fats, such as fish, avocados, eggs or yoghurt.

Listen to your body and eat when you are hungry, but avoid overeating before games and competitions as this can cause discomfort and slow you down.

Avoid sugary and processed foods, which can lead to energy crashes and fatigue during sport.

Stay hydrated by drinking plenty of water throughout the day and during games or competitions.

Avoid skipping meals or restricting food intake, as this can lead to fatigue, weakness and poor performance.

Eat a light meal 2-3 hours before a game or competition to provide energy without it being difficult to digest.

Include fibre in your meals to have energy, stay clear-headed and ready for action! It can help your stomach feel good and help with concentration during sport.

Never drink energy drinks. It could increase your heart rate and blood pressure and even cause anxiety. Water is the best alternative.

Disclaimer: The information provided on this page is for general guidance only and should not be considered medical or professional advice. Always consult a qualified healthcare professional or dietitian for personalised recommendations.

GAME-CHANGING FOOD

Write down your favourite game-changing meals for training day

TRAINING DAY FAVOURITES

Breakfast

Before training:

After training:

Favourite snacks on training day:

GAME-CHANGING FOOD

Write down your favourite game-changing meals for match day

GAME OR COMPETITION DAY FAVOURITES

Breakfast

Before a game/ competition:

After game/ competition:

Favourite snacks on a game/ competition day:

FITTING IT ALL IN

Sometimes you might find it a challenge to fit in training, matches/competitions, school work, family and friends, especially if all of these mean a lot to you. With a little planning and prioritising, it is possible to fit everything in. Here are a few things that can help you achieve this:

Stay positive and motivated
Remember why you love what you do and what your goals are. Stay focused and motivated, and don't let the challenges of balancing everything put you off doing it.

Prioritise
It's important to prioritise your commitments and make sure that you are deciding what you need to spend your time on. Priorities might change throughout the sporting year.

Be effecient
Try to make the most of your time. Maybe use travel time to revise or listen to useful podcasts. Find nuggets of time to do work, such as during free periods at school.

Take care of yourself
Make sure to look after yourself, such as getting enough sleep, eating well and taking breaks when you need them. It's important to avoid doing too much and to take care of your physical and mental well-being.

Communicate with your friends
Let your friends know about your sporting schedule and how important it is to you. They may be more understanding if you miss a social event because of sport.

Make a schedule
Plan your time to include schoolwork, training, matches/competitions and time with friends and family. This will help you stay organised and make sure you are dedicating enough time to each area of your life.

Remember, you're not alone in this journey. If you ever feel overwhelmed, don't hesitate to reach out to your teammates, parents or coach for guidance and support. Together, you can overcome any life challenges and keep pursuing your dreams. You've got a whole team behind you!

RECOVERY, REST AND HAVING FUN

Remember, sport is just one part of your life and, although it means the world to you, it's important to take care of your body, mind and overall well-being both before and after you do it.

Rest

Make sure you get enough sleep each night (about 8-10 hours, depending on your age) and take rest days in between training and games/competitions. This helps your body and mind recharge so you can perform at your best. Going to bed early has so many benefits!

Recovery

Resting will allow your body to recover from the stress and strain of training and competing. This, in turn, will help prevent injuries and burnout. Don't forget, your team needs you on top form!

Fun

Try to have other interests outside of sport. This can help you keep a healthy balance and stop burnout. Spend time with family or pursue other interests, like music, art or reading, where you can conserve your energy and chill out.

THE FUN AWARDS

Write down or draw your 3 most favourite ways to have fun outside of training, matches and competitions.

MY ULTIMATE FAVOURITE WAY TO HAVE FUN IS:

MY 2ND FAVOURITE WAY TO HAVE FUN IS:

MY 3RD FAVOURITE WAY TO HAVE FUN IS:

"Of course, I want to be number one. But being happy and healthy is the most important thing"

Venus Williams

Sport:
Tennis

Team/Country:
USA

Honours:
7 x Grand Slam Singles Titles

MY SHOUT-OUTS

SHOUT-OUTS

It's time to shout out to the people you admire. This could be teammates, players, coaches, or well-known athletes you look up to the most. If you like, you could tell them by sending them a message, whether it's through a heartfelt note, an email or a message on social media. Share specific reasons why you look up to them and let them know the positive influence they've had on your own sports journey. Your words of appreciation can be a source of motivation and encouragement for both you and the person you shout-out to.

Shout-out to:

My teammate, Jo.

Something awesome they did in a match/ training/ competition:

They helped explain something I didn't understand.

Why you appreciate them:

They are always positive and supportive to me when I'm a bit down.

Shout-out to:

Something awesome they did in a match/ training/ competition:

Why you appreciate them:

Shout-out to:

Something awesome they did in a match/ training/ competition:

Why you appreciate them:

Shout-out to:

Something awesome they did in a match/ training/ competition:

Why you appreciate them:

Shout-out to:

Something awesome they did in a match/ training/ competition:

Why you appreciate them:

Shout-out to:

Something awesome they did in a match/ training/ competition:

Why you appreciate them:

Shout-out to:

Something awesome they did in a match/ training/ competition:

Why you appreciate them:

Shout-out to:

Something awesome they did in a match/ training/ competition:

Why you appreciate them:

GAME CHANGER COMMUNITY

You are now part of the Game Changer Sports Journal Community.

Where in the world are you? Share your **#GCsportsjournal** with the Game Changer Community online.

For more information about Game Changer Journals visit our website at **gamechangerjournals.com** and follow us on instagram **@game_changer_journals**.

For exciting updates, new releases and insider insights, join our mailing list at **gamechangerjournals@gmail.com**.

No pages left? When this journal is full, grab your next journal from our website and continue your epic journaling journey.

This journal is a tool, and you are the architect of your success. Keep the momentum going, keep scribbling away, stay connected and continue to write your story.

THANK YOU

This journal would not have been possible without the involvement of some REAL Game Changers. Big thanks to the following people for their contribution:

Luella G

Maceo G

Inaya B

Ella E

Marli-Rae F

Chris McDonald

Alison Neves

Dr. Gabriella Beckles-Raymond

Mathilda Blowers

Jack - 1901 Agency

Feedback

Missing something? Your thoughts matter! We'd love to hear what you think about this journal. If you have suggestions, feedback, or anything you'd like to share, feel free to email us at **gamechangerjournals@gmail.com**. Your input helps us make it even better for the next edition.

"What is a game changer?
A sportsperson who makes
a difference. Known for their
exceptional ability and attitude
to influence a positive outcome"

Zoë & Laura at Game Changer Journals